A Ship Is Coming!

Dennis Fertig
Illustrated by Bradley Clark
and Cynthia Clark

Rigby®
A Harcourt Achieve Imprint

www.Rigby.com
1-800-531-5015

Two friends, Mito and Ramiro, lived on a beautiful island. The young men dreamed of gold and jewels. One summer day, Mito and Ramiro went to the top of a mountain on the island. They looked through a telescope and carefully searched the sea. After a few minutes Ramiro said, "I think I see something far away."

"It's a large ship sailing to our island!" exclaimed Mito. "Maybe it's bringing treasure."

The friends returned to their village.

The next day, Mito went back up the mountain with the telescope. He wanted to watch the ship as it came closer. As Mito looked at the ship, he thought about the treasures it carried. With it he could build a big house, buy beautiful clothes, and eat the best food. He could marry a wonderful woman and have a happy family, too.

Ramiro wanted to be rich just like Mito, but he stayed in the village to find a job. He found a job as a baker's helper. Ramiro learned to bake. He knew that someday he would be a good baker and have his own bakery.

Mito found some wood and
made a chair. He wanted to
have a place to sit while
he watched the ship.
He looked out at the
sea and waited.

In the village, Ramiro worked hard. He was
happy with his work. Ramiro met a smart young
woman named Sarita, and they fell in love.

Mito sat on the mountain staring through the telescope for hours every day. He sat for many days and weeks. Sometimes the ship seemed close, and other times it seemed far away. Mito waited and waited for the ship because he dreamed of treasure.

One day Ramiro and
Sarita got married. Many
people came to their
wedding because they
had lots of friends.
They were
very happy.

A year later, Mito watched as the ship seemed to turn toward the island. As weeks passed, he sat and watched the ship.

Month after month, Mito stared out at the sea.

Ramiro and Sarita liked baking and working together. Soon they opened their own bakery in the village. Many people came to their bakery and their business grew.

As he saw the ship getting closer, Mito jumped up. In his excitement, he dropped the telescope. It fell and smashed on the rocks below. Even without a telescope, Mito could see that the ship was still far away. But he kept waiting.

Ramiro and Sarita lived in a large
house with a beautiful garden. Ramiro
and Sarita's first child was born. Over many
years, their happiness and their family grew.

It was a clear, calm day when Mito saw the ship arriving at the village harbor. Finally his dreams of treasure would come true! He raced down the mountain.

As Mito entered the village he shouted, "The ship is here!" Then Mito ran to meet the ship, but it wasn't a ship! It was just logs and some seaweed! Mito cried because he knew that he had been very foolish to wait for years.

Ramiro and his family went to the harbor.

Mito saw them and said, "My goodness, time has passed, Ramiro. You have a beautiful wife and children!"

Ramiro and Sarita invited Mito to come to their house for dinner.

Later that day, Mito sat with Ramiro and Sarita in their home. He looked at their four children and at the fine meal on the table.

Mito thought about the years that he had wasted.

"Children," said Mito sadly, "do not make my mistake. Do not stop living your life for a foolish dream."